GEORGE FRIDERIC HANDEL

Friedrich

MESSIAH

AN ORATORIO
FOR FOUR SOLO VOICES, CHORUS AND ORCHESTRA

REVISED AND EDITED FROM THE AUTOGRAPH SCORE
AND THE PARTS AT THE FOUNDLING HOSPITAL IN LONDON
BY

ARNOLD SCHERING AND KURT SOLDAN

VOCAL SCORE BY

KURT SOLDAN

C. F. PETERS

FRANKFURT · LONDON · NEW YORK

54142

DER MESSIAS

MESSIAH

ORATORIUM

AN ORATORIO

Für vier Solostimmen ⟨Sopran, Alt, Tenor, Baß⟩, Chor und Orchester von	For four Solo Voices ⟨Soprano, Alto, Tenor, Bass⟩, Chorus and Orchestra by

G. F. HANDEL

Komponiert im Jahre 1741. Zum ersten Male aufgeführt am 13. April 1742 zu Dublin unter Leitung des Komponisten.	Composed in the year 1741. Performed for the first time on April 13, 1742 in Dublin, the composer conducting.

ORCHESTERBESETZUNG / INSTRUMENTATION

2 Oboi — 2 Fagotti
2 Trombe
Timpani
Violino I — Violino II — Viola — Violoncello — Contrabasso
Cembalo — Organo

Die Oboen (mit Ausnahme von Nr. 37) und die Fagotte sind nur in den Originalstimmen (siehe Vorwort der-Partitur, Ed. Peters, Nr. 4500) enthalten, nicht aber in der autographen Partitur.	The parts for oboes — with exception of No. 37 — and bassoons are included only in the original orchestral parts (see Foreword in the score Peters' Ed. No. 4500), not in the autograph score.

Orchestra material available

Suggestions for a shortened version of MESSIAH: see Appendix, p. 205

INTRODUCTION

Handel composed his oratorio "Messiah" in 1741, in the 56th year of his very full and varied life. It received its first performance the following year in Dublin, the capital of Ireland. Handel had been invited by three charity institutions to give concerts there, and had promised to bring with him "some of his best music". The result was magnificent beyond measure. The charities benefited by no less than £400. Since that time the "Messiah" has held a place among the most popular works not only in England but throughout the cultured world. It first came to Germany via Hamburg in 1772, here again acclaimed as a masterpiece, and arranged for performance (at Vienna) by no less a person than Mozart.

The score was completed in 22 days — that is, in little more than three weeks. From reports of his close associates at that time we learn that Handel wrote the work in a mood of highest exaltation, at times seeming almost to be transported beyond the limits of earth. "I did think I did see all Heaven before me — and the great God himself!" he is said to have exclaimed, his face streaming with tears, when he had just completed the second part of the oratorio with the Hallelujah chorus.

Some of the most beautiful and profound passages from the Old and New Testaments were chosen to extol the redeeming deed of Christ. After the serious note sounded by the Overture, in E minor, Part One begins with mighty words of promise, comforting in their certainty. Grand and jubilant choruses and lovely arias prepare for the coming of the Messiah. Immediately after the B minor of the last bass aria "The people that walked in darkness", which seems to feel its way about gropingly, the chorus announces the Birth in a radiant G major. The shepherds come to the manger with tender music, the "Gloria" of the angels rings out, and in tones of utmost bliss — every piece known and loved the world over and a proof of Handel's heaven-born creative powers — the blessing of the healing message is proclaimed. — Part Two is pervaded with the spirit of the Passion and Resurrection. At the beginning there comes the sharply rhythmical summons "Behold the Lamb of God", then the Alto aria "He was despised", which takes one's breath away with its desolate sighs and its description of the scourging. The recitatives pertaining to the agony of Christ are couched in tones of deepest compassion, a blend of sorrow and burning reproach, as in the movement "Thy rebuke hath broken His heart", with its continuation "Behold, and see if there be any sorrow". Handel passes quickly over the Cross and Passion however, as if with a bleeding heart. More important to him than the portrayal of these stern events is the pondering upon the idea of salvation arising out of this suffering. This has been illustrated already by the great fugue "And with His stripes" and the chorus "All we like sheep", so descriptive of the straying aside of a divided humanity. With the chorus "Lift up your heads" the scene changes. The Resurrection is accomplished, hosts of angels await the Messiah, the heavens open and rank upon rank of Cherubim and Seraphim receive Him. A pure, clear F major breaks the spell of the foregoing minor keys. Everything that now follows is the fruit of genius of the highest order, and one can readily believe in the reality of Handel's vision of the heavens in their glory. Not everything is consigned to the chorus. The soprano soloist sings of the beauty of the messengers of the Gospel, the bass sings of the raging of the heathen. And now begins the Hallelujah chorus — the chorus which in England receives such veneration, and during which the audience stand, as when the Gospel is read in church. The harmonic scheme of the movement could hardly be simpler: it consists almost entirely of D major and A major. But the melody and rhythm, the variety of choral texture and the crystal-clear form of the movement combine to produce a monumental effect which overpowers one anew at each hearing. — Part Three is concerned with death and the Last Judgment. Many passages of mystic and esoteric significance from the First Epistle to the Corinthians and the Apocalypse of St. John are contained in it. The aria "I know that my Redeemer liveth", with which it opens, shares with the Hallelujah chorus the honour of immortality. This is due not only to its sublime melody, but equally to the qualities of soul inherent in it — purity, innocence, faith and trust — all reduced to the simplest form imaginable with the touch of a master hand. In contrast we have a little later on the mighty bass aria "The trumpet shall sound" with its allusions to the Day of Judgment. And when, after the solemn pronouncement "Worthy is the Lamb" the fanfare-like theme "Blessing and honour, glory and power" begins, and when finally the whole volume of choral sound merges into the fugal Amen chorus, then the listener, of whatever faith or philosophy of life, stands as it were spellbound by a vision which leads us up to the loftiest heights, but which at the same time strengthens us and raises us up above our selves.

ARNOLD SCHERING

ZUR EINFÜHRUNG

Händel schuf sein Oratorium „Der Messias" im Jahre 1741, im 56. Jahre seines wechsel=
vollen Künstlerlebens. Ein Jahr später kam es in Dublin, der Hauptstadt Irlands, zur ersten
Aufführung. Händel war von drei Wohltätigkeitsinstituten zu Konzerten dahin eingeladen
worden und hatte versprochen, etwas „von seiner besten Musik" mitzubringen. Der Erfolg
war über die Maßen großartig. Nicht weniger als 400 Pfund konnten dem wohltätigen Zweck
zugeführt werden. Seitdem gehört „Der Messias" zu den volkstümlichsten Werken nicht nur in
England, sondern in der ganzen gebildeten Welt. Erst 1772 kam er über Hamburg nach
Deutschland, auch hier als Meisterwerk begrüßt und von keinem Geringeren als Mozart
einer Bearbeitung ⟨für Wien⟩ gewürdigt.

In 22 Tagen — also in etwas mehr als drei Wochen — wurde die Partitur niedergeschrieben.
Aus Berichten derer, die dem Komponisten damals nahestanden, erfahren wir, daß Händel
das Werk in einer grenzenlosen Hochstimmung schuf, in Stunden, die fast einer Erdentrückt=
heit gleichkamen. „Ich glaubte den Himmel offen und den Schöpfer aller Dinge selbst zu
sehen", soll er tränenüberströmt ausgerufen haben, als er den zweiten Teil des Oratoriums
mit dem Halleluja beendet hatte.

Das Erlösungswerk Christi zu verherrlichen, sind die schönsten, tiefsinnigsten Sprüche des
Alten und Neuen Testaments ausgewählt. Mit mächtigen Worten der Verheißung, mit tröst=
lichen der Gewißheit beginnt, nachdem die ernste e moll=Ouverture verrauscht, der erste
Teil. Feierliche Chorklänge und liebliche Arien bereiten auf das Kommen des Messias vor.
Unmittelbar nach der letzten, dem wie tastend herumirrenden h moll=Baßstück „Das Volk,
das da wandelt im Dunkel", verkündet der Chor in hellem D dur die Geburt. Die Hirten
kommen mit zarter Krippenmusik, das Gloria der Engel ertönt, und in tief beseligten Klängen —
jedes Stück weltberühmt und ein Zeugnis begnadeter Schöpferkraft — wird vom Segen der
Heilsbotschaft berichtet. — Der zweite Teil steht unter dem Zeichen der Passion und Auf=
erstehung. Am Anfang der scharf rhythmisierte Anruf an das Gotteslamm und die atem=
versetzende Altarie „Er ward verschmähet" mit ihren einsamen Seufzern und der Geißel=
schilderung. Die Rezitative, die der Marter Christi gewidmet sind, enthalten Töne tiefsten
Mitleids, gemischt aus Trauer und lodernder Empörung, — so der Satz „Diese Schmach brach
ihm sein Herz" mit dem anschließenden „Schau hin und sieh, wer kennet solche Qualen".

Schnell aber, wie mit blutendem Herzen, geht Händel über Kreuz und Leiden hinweg. Wichtiger als· der grauenvolle Passionsvorgang ist ihm die Betrachtung der Heilsidee, die aus diesem Leiden erblüht. Ihr galt bereits die große Fuge „Durch seine Wunden sind wir geheilt" und der Chorsatz „Der Herde gleich" mit der Schilderung des Dahinirrens der gespaltenen Menschheit. Mit dem „Hoch tut euch auf" ändert sich der Schauplatz. Die Auferstehung ist vollzogen, Scharen von Engeln erwarten den Messias, der Himmel öffnet sich, und Cherubim und Seraphim stellen sich zum Empfang auf. Reines F dur löst den Bann früherer Molltonarten. Alles, was jetzt folgt, bedeutet höchste Genieleistung und läßt in der Tat glauben, daß Händel die Vision einer Himmelsglorie gehabt hat. Nicht alles ist dem Chor übergeben. Den lieblichen Schritt der Himmelsboten besingt ein Solosopran, das Toben der Heiden ein Baß. Und dann beginnt· das Halleluja, — dieses Halleluja, das in England nahezu göttliche Verehrung genießt und ⟨wie das Evangelium in der Kirche⟩ von den Hörern stehend mitangehört wird. Die harmonische Einfachheit des Satzes kann nicht weiter getrieben werden: fast nur D dur und A dur. Aber die Melodik und Rhythmik, die Gruppierung der Chorstimmen, die kristallklare Form des Satzes geben ihm eine Wirkung, deren Monumentalität immer von neuem überwältigt. — Der dritte Teil knüpft an Tod und Jüngstes Gericht an. Viel Mystisches, Geheimnisvolles aus dem 1. Korintherbrief und der Offenbarung Johannis steckt in ihm. Die Erlöserarie, die an der Spitze steht, teilt mit dem Halleluja den Ruhm der Unsterblichkeit. Sie verdankt ihn nicht nur der edlen Melodik allein, sondern ebenso den in ihr schwingenden Gemütswerten, dem Reinen, Keuschen, Gläubigen, Zuversichtlichen, — alles auch hier mit letzter Meisterschaft auf das denkbar Einfachste zurückgeführt. Als Gegenstück erscheint ein wenig später die mächtige Baßarie „Sie schallt, die Posaune" mit der Andeutung des Letzten Gerichts. Und wenn dann nach dem feierlichen Spruche „Würdig ist das Lamm" das Fanfarenthema „Alle Gewalt und Preis und Macht" einsetzt und schließlich der ganze Chorstrom in die Amenfuge einmündet, dann steht der Hörer, gleichgültig welchen Bekenntnisses und welcher Lebensanschauung, unter dem Banne einer Erscheinung, die uns zu letzter Erhabenheit hinaufführt, aber gleichzeitig stärkt und über uns selbst erhebt.

ARNOLD SCHERING

INHALT / CONTENTS

ERSTER TEIL / PART THE FIRST

DRITTER TEIL / PART THE THIRD

DER MESSIAS
MESSIAH

Erster Teil
Part the First

Sinfony

Georg Friedrich Händel
(1685-1759)

2

11425

to p 31

1 Accompagnato

Larghetto e piano

Tenore

En-de   und ih-re Mis-se-tat ver-ge-ben,   und ih-re Mis-se-tat ver-ge-
complish'd,   that her in-i-qui-ty   is   pardon'd,   that her in-i-ty is par-

ben.   Vernehmt die Stimme des Predigers in der
don'd.   The voice of him   that crieth   in the

Wü-ste: Be-rei-tet dem Herrn den Weg,   und   eb-net durch Wildnis ihm Pfade, unserm Gott.
wilderness: Pre-pare ye the way of the Lord, make straight in the des-ert a highway for our God.

2 Aria

Andante

Fg. Vl. Vla.
Cont. Cemb.

11425

11425

3 Chorus
Allegro

11425

12

350 Friday

4 Accompagnato

Recitativo Basso

B. So spricht der Herr, Gott Ze-ba-oth: Noch ei-ne klei-ne
Thus saith the Lord, the Lord of Hosts: Yet once, a lit-tle

Vl.Vla.
Cont.
Cemb.

5
B. Zeit, und ich be - weg___ den
while, and I will shake___ the

8
B. Him-mel und die Er-de, das Meer und das Trockne, und ich be - weg,___
heav'ns and the earth, the sea and the dry land, and I will shake,___

11
B. und ich be - weg___
and I will shake___

14
B. die Mensch-heit, es bebt der Him - mel, die
all na - tions; I'll shake the heav'ns, the

5 Aria

Larghetto

Doch wer wird er - tra - gen den Tag sei - ner An - kunft,
But who may a - bide the day of His com - ing,

und wer be - steht, wenn Er er - schei - net, wer be - steht,
and who shall stand when He ap - pear - eth, who shall stand

wenn Er er - schei - net, doch wer wird er - tra - gen, doch wer wird er -
when He ap - pear - eth, but who may a - bide, but who may a -

tra - gen den Tag sei - ner An - kunft, und wer be - steht, wenn Er er -
bide the day of His com - ing, and who shall stand when He ap -

11425

24

26

11425

7 Recitativo

Alto

Denn sieh, der Ver-hei-ße-ne des Herrn er-scheint auf Er-den,
Be-hold, a vir-gin shall con-ceive, and bear a son,

und sein Na-me heißt E-ma-nu-el, „Gott mit uns."
and shall call his name Em-ma-nu-el, "God with us."

Cont.
Cemb.

8 **Aria**

Andante

9 **Chorus**

attacca il Coro

10 Accompagnato

Andante larghetto

38

11 Aria

Larghetto

Basso

to p 75

12 Chorus

Andante allegro

11425

46

11425

13 Pifa

Larghetto e mezzo piano

14 Recitativo

Soprano

Es wa-ren Hir-ten bei-sammen auf dem Felde, die_ hü-te-ten ih - re Herden des Nachts.
There were shepherds a - bid-ing in the field, keeping watch over their flock by night.

Cont.
Cemb.

Accompagnato

Andante

Und sie-he, der En - gel des Herrn trat zu ih-nen,
And lo, the an-gel of the Lord came up-on them

Vl.Vla.
Cont.
Cemb. *p*

und die Klar - heit des Herrn um - leuchte-te sie, und sie fürchteten sich sehr.
and the glo-ry of the Lord shone round a - bout them, and they were sore a-fraid.

12 Recitativo

Und der En-gel sprach zu ih-nen: Fürch - tet euch nicht! Ich brin-ge fro-he
And the an-gel said un-to them: Fear not; for be-hold, I bring you good

Cont.
Org.

15 Chorus

16 Aria

Allegro

Fg.
Vl. unis.
Cont. Cemb.

Soprano

S. Erwach, er-wach, er-wach,__froh-lo-cke, froh-lo-
Re-joice, re-joice, re-joice____ greatly, re-joice,____

S. -cke, o Toch-ter von Zi-on,
O daugh-ter of Zi-on,

S. o Toch-ter von Zi-on, er-wach,_____ froh-lo-
O daugh-ter of_ Zi-on, re-joice,_____ re-joice,_____

60

Edition Peters   11425

11425

er- wach,— froh - lo - cke, o Toch- ter von Zi - on, jauch -
re - joice ___ great-ly, O daugh-ter of Zi - on, shout, ___

ze, du Toch- ter von Je - ru - sa - lem, blick auf, dein Kö - nig kommt zu
__ O daugh-ter of Je - ru-sa-lem, be - hold, thy King cometh un - to

dir, blick auf, dein Kö - nig kommt zu dir.
thee, be - hold, thy King com-eth un - to thee.

64

Edition Peters   11425

11425

Das Rezitativ Nr.17 und das Larghetto Nr.18 sind noch in folgender späteren Fassung vorhanden:

There is another later version of the Recitative No.17 and the Larghetto No.18 reading as follows:

17a Recitativo
Alto

Dann wird das Au-ge des Blinden sich auf-tun, und das Ohr des Tauben wird hö-ren; dann
Then shall the eyes of the blind be op-en'd, and the ears of the deaf un-stop-ped; then

spring-et der Lah-me wie ein Hirsch, und die Zun-ge des Stum-men wird sin-gen.
shall the lame man leap as an hart, and the tongue of the dumb shall sing.

18a Duetto
Larghetto e piano
Alto

Er
He

weidet sei-ne Her-de, dem Hir - ten gleich, und he-get sei-ne Lämmer so sanft in seinem Arm, — so
shall feed His flock like a shep - - herd, and He — shall ga-ther the lambs with His arm,

sanft in sei-nem Arm, er wei-det sei-ne Her-de, dem Hir - ten gleich, und
with His — arm, He shall feed His flock like a shep - - herd, and

Edition Peters   11425

11425

19 Chorus

Zweiter Teil
Part the Second

20 Chorus

76

Edition Peters   11425

78

Den Rü-cken bot er den Pei-ni-gern,
He gave His back to the smi - ters,

den Rü-cken bot er den Pei-ni-gern, hielt die Wan - ge
He gave His back to the smi - ters, and His cheeks to

dar der ro - hen Fein - de Wut, hielt dar die
them that pluck - ed off the hair, and His cheeks to

[Fine]

to p 82

da capo [al Fine]

22 Chorus

Largo e staccato

11425

23 Chorus

24 Chorus

25 Accompagnato

Larghetto

26 Chorus

11425

100

27 Accompagnato

Largo Tenore

28 Arioso

Largo e piano

29 Accompagnato

Recitativo

30 Aria

Andante larghetto

Doch du ließest ihn im Gra - be nicht,
But Thou didst not leave His soul in hell,
doch du lie - ßest ihn im
but Thou didst not leave His

Gra - be nicht; du woll-test nicht dulden, du wolltest nicht dulden, daß dein Hei - li - ger Ver-
soul in hell; nor didst Thou suf-fer, nor didst Thou suf-fer Thy Ho-ly One to

we - sung sä - he,
see cor-ruption,
doch du lie - ßest ihn im
but Thou didst not leave His

Gra - be nicht, du lie - ßest ihn, du lie - ßest ihn im Gra - be nicht;
soul in hell, Thou didst not leave, Thou didst not leave His soul in hell;

31 Chorus

A tempo ordinario

11425

114

78

ist der Kö-nig der Eh-ren, er ist der Kö-nig der Eh-ren, der Eh - ren.
is the King of Glo-ry, He is the King of Glo-ry, of Glo - ry.

ist der Kö - nig der Eh-ren, er ist der Kö - nig der Eh-ren, der Eh - ren.
is the King of Glo-ry, He is the King of Glo-ry, of Glo - ry.

ist der Kö - nig der Eh-ren, er ist der Kö - nig der Eh-ren, der Eh - ren.
is the King of Glo-ry, He is the King of Glo-ry, of Glo - ry.

ist der Kö - nig der Eh-ren, er ist der Kö - nig der Eh-ren, der Eh - ren.
is the King of Glo-ry, He is the King of Glo-ry, of Glo - ry.

73

32 Recitativo

Tenore

T.

Zu welchem von den Engeln hat jemals er ge-sagt: Du bist mein Sohn, und heut hab ich ge-zeuget dich?
Un-to which of the angels said He at a-ny time: Thou art My Son, this day have I be-gotten Thee?

Cont.
Org.

33 Chorus

Allegro

Sopr.

Laßt al-le En-gel des Herrn prei - sen ihn, laßt
Let all the an-gels of God wor - ship Him, let

Alto

Laßt al-le En-gel des Herrn prei - sen ihn, laßt al-le
Let all the an-gels of God wor - ship Him, let all the

Ten.

Laßt al-le En-gel des Herrn prei - sen ihn,
Let all the an-gels of God wor - ship Him,

Basso

Laßt al-le En-gel des Herrn prei - sen ihn,
Let all the an-gels of God wor - ship Him,

Allegro

Ob. Fg. Vl. Vla.
Cont. Cemb. Org.

116

Edition Peters   11425

woh - - ne, stets woh - - - - - - - - -
dwell a - mong them, might dwell _____

- - - ne ___ bei ih - nen,   daß Gott stets woh - ne bei ih - nen. [144]
a - mong them,   that the Lord God might dwell a - mong them.

Dieselbe Arie wurde von Händel für Alt in folgender | Handel's version of this Aria for Alto reads as follows:
Fassung aufgezeichnet:

34a Aria

Allegro larghetto

Fg.
Vl. unis.
Cont. Cemb.

126

35 Chorus

Andante allegro

Sopr.
Groß war die Menge der Boten Got-tes, groß war die Men - - -
Great was the compa-ny of the preachers, great was the com -

Alto
Groß war die Menge der Boten Got-tes, groß war die Men - ge, die
Great was the compa-ny of the preachers, great was the com - pa-ny, the

Ten.
Der Herr gab das Wort: Groß war die Menge der Boten Got-tes, groß war die Men - ge, die
The Lord gave the word: great was the compa-ny of the preachers, great was the com - pa-ny, the

Basso
Der Herr gab das Wort: Groß war die Menge der Boten Got-tes, groß war die Men - -
The Lord gave the word: great was the compa-ny of the preachers, great was the com - -

Andante allegro

Ob.Fg.Vl.
Vla.Cont.Cemb.Org.

- - ge der Bo-ten Got - tes,
pa-ny of the prea - chers,

Men - ge, die Men - - - ge, die Men-ge der Bo-ten Got - tes,
com - pa-ny, the com - pa-ny, the com-pa-ny of the prea - chers,

Men - - ge, die Men - - ge der Bo-ten Got - tes,
com - - pa-ny, the com - pa-ny of the prea - chers,

- - ge, die Men - - - ge der Bo-ten Got - tes,
- pa-ny, the com - pa-ny of the prea - chers,

11425

Die vorstehende Arie ist auch in der folgenden Fassung für Alt vorhanden, der sich an Stelle des Chores Nr. 37 das Tenor-Solo Nr. 87a anschloß:

The above aria is also extant in the following version for alto, which preceded the tenor solo No. 87a in place of Chorus No. 37:

Die autographe Partitur enthält vorstehende Arie noch in folgender späteren Bearbeitung für Sopran- und Alt-Solo mit Chor:

The autograph score contains the above aria as well in the following later arrangement for soprano and alto solo with chorus:

36 b Soli e Chorus

135

Edition Peters   11425

11425

Die folgende (dritte) Fassung des gleichen Textes wurde von Händels Kopisten Christoph Schmidt in die autographe Partitur nachgetragen. Dieser Fassung ging die Arie Nr. 86b voraus.

The following (third) version of the same text was added to the autograph score by Handel's copist Christoph Schmidt. This version followed Aria No. 36b.

37a Arioso

Andante larghetto

38 Aria

Allegro

150

Die vorstehende Arie hat Händel noch in folgender stark
gekürzten Fassung unter Hinzufügung eines neuen rezi-
tativischen Schlusses aufgezeichnet. Diese Fassung geben auch die Stimmen an.

The above aria was given by Handel also in the following
much abbreviated version with the addition of a new
ending in recitative form. The choral and orchestral
parts correspond also to this version.

38a Aria

Allegro

34

B. Rat, die Völ - - - - - - ker stol - zen
thing, im ag - - - - - - ine a vain

37

B. Rat?
thing.?
Die Kön-ge der Welt stehn auf, und die
The kings of the earth rise up, and the

41

B. Fürsten entflammen in Aufruhr wi-der den Herrn und seinen Ge - salb - - - ten.
ru-lers take counsel to-ge-ther against the Lord and His a - noint - - - ed.

39 Chorus

Allegro e staccato

Sopr. Auf, zer-rei-ßet ih - re Ban-de, auf, zer - reißt,
Let us break their bonds a - sun-der, let us break,

Alto Auf, zer-rei-ßet ih - re Ban-de, auf, zer-
Let us break their bonds a - sun-der, let us

Ten. Auf, zer-rei-ßet ih - re Ban-de, auf, zer-rei-ßet sie, zer-rei - ßet ih - re Ban-de, auf, zer-
Let us break their bonds a - sunder, let us, let us break their bonds a - sunder, let us, let us

Basso Auf, zer rei-ßet ih - re Ban-de, auf, zer-rei-ßet,
Let us break their bonds a - sun-der, let us, let us

Allegro e staccato

Ob. Fg. Vl. Vla.
Cont. Cemb. Org.

154

11425

158

41 Aria

Andante

55

T. —pfers Ge - fä - ße, wie des Tö - pfers Ge - fä - ße,   du zer - brichst sie zu
—ter's ves - sel, like a pot - ter's ves - sel,   *Thou shalt dash them in*

61

T. Scher - ben   wie des Tö - - - - pfers Ge - fä - ße. [182]
pie - ces   *like a pot - - - - - ter's ves - sel.*

66

70

Das folgende unmittelbar an Nr. 40 sich anschließende Rezitativ hat zeitweilig an Stelle der Arie Nr. 41 gestanden:	The following recitative, immediately preceded by No. 40, stood at times in place of Aria No. 41:

41a Recitativo

Tenore

T. Du zerschlägst sie mit dem Eisenzepter,   du zerbrichst sie zu Scherben wie des Töpfers Ge-fä-ße.
Thou shalt break them with a rod of i - ron,   *Thou shalt dash them to pie-ces like a pot-ter's vessel.*

Cont.
Cemb.

42 Chorus

Allegro

168

Dritter Teil
Part the Third

43 Aria

Ich weiß, daß mein Er - lö - ser le - bet,
I know that my Re - deem - er liv - eth,

und daß er er - scheint_____ am__ letz - - ten__
and that He shall stand_____ at__ the lat - - ter__

Ta - - - - - ge die - ser Erd,
day_____ up - on the earth,

45 Accompagnato

Vernehmt, ich künd ein Geheimnis an: Wir ent-schlafen nicht alle, doch werden wir alle ver-

Be-hold, I tell you a mys-te-ry; we shall not all sleep, but we shall all be

wandelt, und das plötzlich, in des Au-gen-blickes Wehn, beim Schall der Po - sau-ne.

chang'd, in a mo-ment, in the twinkling of an eye, at the last trumpet.

46 Aria

Pomposo, ma non allegro

11425

180

[131]
B. werden ver - wan - - - - - - - delt, wir werden ver -
shall be chang'd, _____ and we shall be

[138] Adagio [Tempo I]
B. wan-delt, verwan - delt.
chang'd, we shall be chang'd.

[145]

[151] [Fine]

[156]
B. Denn dies Ver - wes - li-che wird er - stehn un - ver - wes-lich, denn
For this cor - rup-ti-ble must put __ on in - cor - rup-tion, for
Cont. Cemb. p

[165]
B. dies Ver-wes - li-che wird er-stehn, wird er-stehn, _____
this cor - rup-ti-ble must put on, must put on, _____
p

Edition Peters   11425

da capo [al Fine]

11425

47 Recitativo

Alto

A. Dann wird er-füllt was da geschrieben stehet: Der Tod ist in den Sieg verschlungen.
Then shall be brought to pass the saying that is written, Death is swallow'd up in vic-to-ry.

Cont.
Cemb.

48 Duetto

Andante

Alto

A. O Tod, o Tod, wo, wo ist dein Sta-chel, Tod, wo ist dein
O death, O death, where, where is thy sting, O death, where is thy

Tenore

T. O Grab, o
O grave, O

Andante

Cont.
Cemb. p

4

A. Stachel, o Grab, wo dei-ne Sie-gesmacht, o Grab, o
sting, O grave, where is thy vic-to-ry, O grave, O

T. Grab, wo, wo dei-ne Sie-gesmacht, wo dei-ne Sie-gesmacht, o Tod,
grave, where, where is thy vic-to-ry, where is thy vic-to-ry, O death,

4

7

A. Tod, o Tod, wo, wo ist dein Stachel, wo, o Grab, wo dei-ne
death, O death, where, where is thy sting, where, O grave, where is thy

T. wo, wo ist dein Stachel, wo, wo ist dein Stachel, o Grab, wo dei-ne
where, where is thy sting, where, where is thy sting, O grave, where is thy

7

49 Chorus

51 Chorus

11425

200

11425

APPENDIX

A shortened version of MESSIAH (approximately 2½ hours in duration) may be performed if certain passages are omitted.

The following is a list of possible deletions:

Sinfony........Measure 12, the repeat

(No.4 Recitative, No.5 Aria and No.6 Chorus)

No.16 Aria.....Measure 69, 2nd quarter to Measure 92, 1st quarter
(2nd quarter: 𝄽 ♪) or Measure 71, 3rd quarter to
Measure 88, 2nd quarter

No.18 Aria.....Measure 26-31, Measure 38-45

No.21 Aria.....Measure 43 to Measure 49, 2nd quarter.
da capo: Measure 1-8 and Measure 12-35

No.23 Chorus...(Measure 27-80)

No.24 Chorus...Measure 35, 3rd quarter to Measure 55, 2nd quarter

No.25 Recitative

No.26 Chorus...Entirely, or Measure 20, 3rd quarter to Measure 48,
2nd quarter

No.31 Chorus...(Measure 34-52)

(No.32 Recitative, No.33 Chorus, No.34 Aria and No.35 Chorus)
or No.33 Chorus and No.34 Aria only

No.39 Chorus...Measure 32-45

No.46 Aria.....Measure 8, 2nd quarter to Measure 20, 1st quarter
Measure 71-108, Measure 156-213

(No.47 Recitative, No.48 Duet, No.49 Chorus and No.50 Aria)
or No.50 Aria only

No.51 Chorus...Measure 39, 4th quarter to Measure 53, 3rd quarter
(with the Alto pausing until Measure 56)

No.52 Chorus...Measure 36-50

N.B. Less desirable deletions are given in parenthesis.

Certain adjustments will be necessitated by the deletion of material as suggested above; these will not be gone into here, since they are self-evident.